Sports Heroes

Who's Clues?

™

By
Nathan Levy

MIND MOTION™

TREND enterprises, Inc.

Introduction

What better way to provide a fun, change of pace than with a Whose Clues?™ book! Not only do you have fun trying to guess the answer, but also you are developing creative, divergent thinking skills.

Each page gives five clues that describe a famous person or character. By listening to each of the clues, asking questions, and working together, players guess the person's or character's identity. Participants will have many chances to develop cooperative learning and deductive thinking skills—without even realizing it. Whose Clues?™ provides unlimited teaching and learning opportunities that kids from ages 8 to 88 love!

How to Use This Book

1. The object is to identify the person or character described by the clues.

2. Choose a reader to read the first clue. Always read only one clue at a time.

3. Remind the players to listen carefully to the clue. After hearing the clue they may ask "yes" or "no" questions and work together to figure out the answer. Answer their questions only with "yes" or "no" responses. Allow adequate time for the questions.

4. Read the next clue and repeat the process until all the clues have been read, or until someone correctly identifies the person or character.

5. If the players are clearly stuck and frustrated after several repetitions, feel free to give them hints.

Who am I?

- I was cut from my high school team in 10th grade.

- My only hero is Tiger Woods.

- I spent some of my retirement in Birmingham.

- Some people think my first name is Air.

- I led the Chicago Bulls to six NBA Championships.

1

Michael Jordan

Who am I?

- My countrymen called me a traitor in 1989.

- My summer in Montreal was perfect.

- I was perfect in my uneven performance.

- I was a member of the Romanian women's gymnastics team.

- I won five gold medals in the Olympics.

Nadia Comaneci

2

Who am I?

- I was born in 1940.

- In my spare time I enjoy designing golf courses.

- I've worn a green jacket more than anyone else in my profession.

- In 1988, I was named Golf Player of the Century.

- My nickname is the Golden Bear.

3

Jack Nicklaus

Who am I?

- I struck gold in 1960.

- My career was put on hold because of a war.

- I am famous for the Thrilla in Manilla.

- I float like a butterfly and sting like a bee.

- I was born Cassius Clay but later changed my name.

Muhammad Ali

4

Who am I?

- I was born in 1895 in Maryland.

- I invented the modern baseball bat.

- Two of my favorite numbers are three and 60.

- The house I built is in New York.

- I was the first professional baseball player to hit 60 home runs.

5

Babe Ruth

Who am I?

- I excel down slopes.

- You have probably said my first name to a baby.

- My last name could be called my road to success.

- I was the fastest woman on the Super G course in the Winter Olympics in Nagano.

- I am the only American—male or female—to win the World Cup downhill crown.

Picabo Street

6

who am I?

- Our track to success began at UCLA.

- Seoul was a golden experience for both of us.

- Though we are not related by blood, we do share a last name.

- I was named after JFK's wife, and my sister-in-law was known as Flo Jo.

- We both have set many world records in track and field.

7

Jackie Joyner-Kersee and
Florence Griffith-Joyner

Who am I?

- I ran further than anyone else in my sport.

- I was elected into the Hall of Fame in 1993.

- I played in the black and blue division, sometimes with broken ribs.

- I was sweetness for the Chicago Bears.

- I currently hold the rushing record in the NFL.

Walter Payton

8

Who am I?

- Ernest Hemingway wanted to take me fishing in *The Old Man and the Sea.*

- "Where have you gone?" is often asked of me.

- Fifty-six is my most memorable number.

- I married a young starlet named Marilyn Monroe.

- I was nicknamed the Yankee Clipper because of my success playing for the New York Yankees.

9 Joe DiMaggio

Who am I?

- There is a hint of royalty in my name.

- I became the first in my position to earn $100,000 in prize money a year.

- My most memorable game was over Bobby; it wasn't rigged.

- Steffi, Martina, and Venus have capitalized from my sweat.

- With my six Wimbledon singles championships and four U.S. Open titles, I changed the world of women's tennis.

Billie Jean King 10

Who am I?

- I started as a Trojan; now, I'm a Cardinal.

- In 1984, I found silver.

- I wear #25 but am most famous for #70.

- Sammy Sosa and I hit a lot of home runs in 1998 and 1999.

- I currently hold the Major League record for most home runs in a season.

11

Mark McGwire

Who am I?

- I started skating when I was two years old.

- My dad was voted "best-known dad" in Canada.

- Gordie Howe is my idol.

- My favorite number #9 was taken, so I decided to wear #99.

- When I was nine years old, I got my nickname The Great One, and it stayed with me throughout my NHL career.

Who am I?

- I'm a team player.

- When you hear my name, you might think that I'm obnoxious.

- I've scored more goals than any other woman.

- I'm a striker, but I don't picket.

- I was a member of the 1999 Women's World Cup Championship team.

13

Mia Hamm

Who am I?

- I was known as the Little Powerhouse.

- Whenever I see a box of Wheaties, I smile.

- My perfect scores vaulted me to the gold.

- Bela was my guru; he helped Nadia too.

- I was the first American woman to win the all-around Olympic gold medal in gymnastics.

Mary Lou Retton

14

Who am I?

- My boyhood idol was Stan Musial.

- I liked playing shortstop, but the Yankees made me play outfield.

- I originally wore #6 but fell into a slump, so I changed to #7.

- I set a record with 18 World Series home runs.

- My nicknames were The Mick and The Switcher.

15

Mickey Mantle

Who am I?

- I was rookie of the year in 1985.

- People sometimes ask me if I have a brother named Luigi.

- I've always been a penguin that likes ice.

- I now own the team I once played for.

- My #66 will never be worn in Pittsburgh again.

Mario Lemieux 16

Who am I?

- I took a test without permission and became a senior.

- My revolutions are chilling.

- My artistry is etched in ice.

- "I didn't lose the gold. I won the silver in Nagano."

- I am considered to be one of the best in figure skating.

17

Michelle Kwan

Who am I?

- I was the first draft pick in 1979.

- My college days were spent chasing a Bird.

- My team was a dream in Barcelona.

- I have a magical nickname, but my real name is Earvin.

- I led the Los Angeles Lakers to several NBA Championships.

Magic Johnson

18

Who am I?

- I didn't start on my varsity football team until my junior year.

- I grew up in the same city as Johnny Unitas and Joe Namath.

- I was picked 82nd overall in the 1979 NFL draft.

- My nickname is the Comeback Kid.

- I won four Super Bowls for the San Francisco 49ers.

19 Joe Montana

Who am I?

- I started my career in New York and finished it in Texas.

- I went to Cooperstown in 1999, with my friends George and Robin.

- I'm the only pitcher to ever throw seven no-hitters.

- I have 5,714 strikeouts, more than anyone who has ever played.

- My nickname is the Ryan Express.

Nolan Ryan 20

who am I?

- I grew up in the Land of Lincoln; it was a cool place to live.

- I was named Sportsman of the Year, even though it doesn't really describe me.

- I eat peanut butter and jelly sandwiches before I skate around.

- When I glided to victory in Lillehammer, I became the most decorated American Winter Olympian.

- I currently hold the speed skating records in the 500- and 1000-meter events.

21

Bonnie Blair

Who am I?

- I appeared on the Mike Douglas Show with my dad.

- I won three amateur titles—more than anyone ever has in my sport.

- I pounced onto the PGA tour at age 20.

- I was the master of my profession in 1997.

- My first name is Eldrick, but you know me by my nickname. My last name is the same as some of the clubs I use.

Tiger Woods

Who am I?

- My favorite singer is Kenny Rogers.

- I was the 1979 college player of the year.

- Though only 2,100 lived in my hometown of French Lick, Indiana, 4,000 always showed up to watch my high school games.

- I played myself in the movie *Blue Chips*.

- I led the Boston Celtics to three NBA Championships.

23

Larry Bird

Who am I?

- I was known as The Black Pearl.

- I hated wearing my braces.

- Although I was lightning fast, I wasn't one of the reindeer.

- I was the first American woman to win three gold medals in one Olympics.

- Before Flo Jo, I was the fastest woman in the world.

Wilma Rudolph

24

Who am I?

- I am the youngest of four children.

- I played tennis against Bjorn Borg when I was four years old.

- My father, an Olympic boxer, taught me how to swing a racquet.

- Winning at Wimbledon in 1992, was one of my favorite memories.

- Turning pro at age 16, I've been playing "Rock 'n Roll Tennis" ever since.

25

Andre Agassi

Who am I?

- A civil war was stopped in Nigeria when I came to town to play.

- My first job was shining shoes, but I always dreamed of playing soccer.

- My real name is Edson Arantes do Nascimento, but I'm best known by one word.

- I am the only player to win three World Cups for my country Brazil.

- At the end of my career, I played soccer for the New York Cosmos.

Pelé

who am I?

- I had 17 national records by age 10.

- I set 32 records in the Olympics.

- In Munich, I won seven gold medals in seven events.

- Once an orthodontist, I now give motivational speeches all over the world.

- I am considered the greatest swimmer of all time.

27

Mark Spitz

Who am I?

- I prefer Coke over Pepsi—
  now that I own a bottling
  company.

- I played in the ABA before
  playing for the NBA.

- I was the first to slam dunk
  a basketball from the free
  throw line.

- A friend in high school gave
  me my Ph.D. nickname.

- I was the doctor of
  my profession for the
  Philadelphia 76ers.

Julius Erving (Dr. J) 28